Foreword

People living in care have faced 14 long months of restrictions on their movement and on contact with those most important to them. Things that we all used to take for granted but recently have come to realise are the basics of a fulfilling life. Care home residents have lived under far stricter restrictions, for much longer, than any other group in society. All because they happen to need support.

Isolation in care is having a devastating impact on people's lives. The Relatives & Residents Association helpline hears of increased distress, anxiety and depression, of residents who think they have been imprisoned or abandoned by their family, who have stopped eating, drinking or taking medication and given up on life.

The Government's response to the pandemic in care homes has swung dramatically between two extremes. Early on, their mantra to 'protect the NHS' led to policies which put care home residents at far greater risk, leaving the sector without even basic protections and residents feeling abandoned. Now, their guidance imposing a blanket 14-day isolation period mandates a wholesale breach of residents' fundamental human rights. Whilst the rest of the country is opening up and regaining freedoms, people living in care have been left behind in the most appalling way.

Their voices have too long been ignored. Their experiences and stories must be heard by those in power. People living in care don't want to just exist, they want to live. We must end isolation in care.

Helen Wildbore, Director of the Relatives and Residents Association

Introduction

How has a country which prides itself on its tolerance, democracy, equality and decency slid into accepting a situation where the people who most need our care have been neglected, mistreated, falsely imprisoned, stripped of their freedom and their rights as citizens and humans? How is it possible that, as the rest of the country comes out of lockdown and people long separated can finally be together again, those who have suffered the most and lost the most over the past fourteen months are, for no logical reason, being shut into rooms in care homes without their consent and left there? Are they not one of us?

The Government's fourteen-day rule is the most recent iteration of its many guidances which over the past year have treated people in homes as lesser than the rest of society. Old people, young people, people who are cognitively impaired and people who are not, people who are at the end of their life and only want to be with those they love have been punished for their vulnerability. Those who love them have been helpless witnesses and now must live with that guilt and unresolved trauma. It dehumanises all of us if we allow such needless sorrow and harm to continue.

The voices in this booklet are eloquent testimonies of anguish and of the cruelty that continues to be inflicted on people in care homes. They demonstrate how at every level the fourteen-day rule is wrong, and they show how in its baffling impracticality it has a series of unintended consequences. People needing to go into care homes may no longer be willing to do so for fear of isolation. People admitted to hospitals from homes can be unwilling to leave because they will have to quarantine (they become inadvertent 'bed blockers' at a time when the NHS is buckling under a backlog of postponed operations). At the same time, residents of homes are choosing not to go into hospital for necessary procedures because it would mean solitary confinement afterwards. Social isolation is not a humane option for many in care homes (the young person with autism, the old person with dementia...), yet it is being imposed on them with devastating results. Isolation units have been set up in homes, where people serve their time in bewilderment and distress.

The stories here are a tiny fraction of the thousands of stories of suffering that the Government has refused to listen to as it grinds out its incoherent, bureaucratic, treacherous guidances. That they have wriggled away from taking responsibility for these guidances is an act of gross irresponsibility and negligence. It has been left to care providers - most of which want to do the right thing but are fearful of legal and financial consequences - to interpret them. While some homes have acted with compassion throughout the pandemic, others have failed to recognise that a home must not be turned into a prison.

Shame on these singularly nasty guidances - and shame on all of us if we continue to think it is OK to abandon a whole section of society to such acute suffering and distress.

Nicci Gerrard, Author of *What Dementia Teaches Us About Love* and Co-founder of John's Campaign

The Holding Pen

14 DAYS ENFORCED ISOLATION
FOR PEOPLE LIVING IN CARE HOMES

"Grandma! I'm finally allowed to see you again!"

John's Campaign

The Holding Pen

14 Days Enforced Isolation for People Living in Care Homes

This booklet is based mainly on testimonies sent directly to John's Campaign or via the Rights for Residents group during the bank holiday weekend 29th-31st May 2021. At this point most of England was on the penultimate stage of the Government's road map: people were able to embrace each other, to spend time together indoors or out, to enjoy sport, entertainment and hospitality in Covid-secure venues, to travel, study, worship, work, and receive medical treatment. Group sizes were limited and people who tested positive for the virus were expected to self-isolate within their households for 10 days.

People who lived in care homes were not part of these freedoms. If they moved into residential care, visited their family home or spent time in hospital they were required to spend 14 days in isolation, regardless of testing. There was no provision for exercise, mental activity or time outside. Many had already endured repeated periods of confinement which they could neither understand nor give consent to. On Friday 28th May 2021 the Government legal department once again dismissed arguments based on equality and human rights. In this booklet families describe the damage that is being done everyday by this inhumane requirement.

We are grateful to Private Eye magazine for permission to reproduce the cartoons by Grizelda and Martin Ross which appeared in the magazine (issues 1546 & 1547).

ISBN 978-1-899262-45-8

Typeset by Bertie Wheen

Proofread by Ruth Elias Jones

Printed by Bettaprint Woodbridge Ltd.

Published by Golden Duck (UK) Ltd.

Sokens
Green Street
Pleshey
nr. Chelmsford
Essex
CM3 1HT

golden-duck.co.uk

Experiences

Section 1

How the 14-day isolation rule prevents people accepting the care they need or traumatises them and their families

From Andrea:

'I have had no respite for 16 months now I'm so so tired and exhausted.'

I'm 49 years old. I look after my husband Michael who was diagnosed with dementia February 2019 at the age of 49 [...] I have had no respite for 16 months now I'm so so tired and exhausted and really need a break [...] I was told my husband could go into respite but would have to have a PCR test 72 hours before he goes to respite and would have to isolate in his room for 14 days [...] I understand having the PCR test before going into respite therefore if you test negative surely there is no need to keep these vulnerable people away from others. I'm therefore reluctant to send my husband to respite because I do not want him stuck in a room on his own.

From Cathy:

'By this time I had had enough, I brought her home at the beginning of May.'

My mum went into a care home at the end of August last year. She has an extremely poor short term memory and it was becoming very difficult to leave her. We live in the country and with the pandemic no-one seemed to have the capacity to provide care at home, I tried several agencies.

Mum was isolated for 14 days on going in which was incredibly stressful for her and, for various reasons, mum has now been isolated for 14 days three times. The second time she became so distressed it resulted in a TIA [a Transient Ischemic Attack / mini stroke] and her going to hospital. After her day in hospital they wanted to isolate her for a further 14 days, I begged them that it would kill her, and eventually, because she has only been a day patient, they relented. Mum's most recent isolation was at the beginning of April, I received a phone call saying that she had tested positive for Covid. She was the only person connected to the home that had tested positive, she had seen no-one apart from my sister and I (behind a screen and we both tested negative) and it was 99.9% a false result, but they refused to test again and isolated her for another 14 days. By this time I had had enough, I brought her home at the beginning of May to spend some time with me. Very reluctantly mum has returned to the care home today, because I am not here to look after her for the next 5 days [...] I am distraught at the thought of yet another 14 days' isolation and what it will do to her [...]

I think I will have to assess things when I return after the 5 days and possibly bring her out again. However I am supposed to be working full time as an accountant, as well as supporting my husband with his business, and have two very active teenage sons that need driving around. It is not easy and I am struggling to cope. I am falling behind with my work, in danger of losing my job and struggling emotionally.

From Helen:

'I could hardly sleep last night for the thought of her having to isolate in her room for two weeks.'

Today, I am moving my 98-year-old mother from her respite care home to her permanent home near where I live. I could hardly sleep last night for the thought of her having to isolate in her room for two weeks. She will feel like a prisoner and I won't be able to help her settle in. I have no doubt that the care home staff will do their best for her but she will be lonely and frightened without me around - they are all strangers to her.

Whilst looking for the right home for her, I have found care home managers to be anxious and inflexible. They cite 'official guidance' and won't enter into a discussion of individual risk. When my mother is moving directly from one care setting to another - she will be in my car with just me for the whole journey - why is it necessary for her to be isolated for two weeks?

At 98, every day counts. My mother's separation from her family, from the contact and reassurance in a bewildering world that she needs the most, is breaking my heart, along with hers. 'What am I being punished for?' she asks me. What, indeed?

Somehow we need to give care home staff the confidence to do what their instincts used to be telling them and to treat each person as an individual whose needs can be met in a balance of risk versus basic human rights. My mother's spiritual needs have gone largely unmet during the last 18 months. Her local church is opening next week under carefully controlled conditions but she won't be allowed to go. There is no sense in these rigid measures in care homes. How can we help them to open their doors again?

From Anne:

'How could we take this lovely but unwell and unhappy man to a place we couldn't see inside, and allow them to amplify his confusion and unhappiness by locking him up?'

My husband had suddenly become startlingly ill more or less overnight on New Year's Day, having lived peacefully with an Alzheimer's diagnosis since 2013. He very suddenly became agitated, deeply confused, restless, shouty and aggressive at night and we had no idea what to do. Eventually we managed to organise Waking Nights care 3 or 4 nights a week, with my two wonderful daughters and me covering the remaining nights; he would get up as many as seven times a night completely confused and disoriented, and was shouty and agitated, sometimes trying to hit carers. We then employed a live-in carer but he disliked her and she couldn't cope and in the end we realised that we were not managing during both the days and nights and he needed more 24 hour care than we could provide.

So we started to look at local care homes, but at that point more or less all we were allowed to do was walk round the outsides of homes, peering through windows, and they all told us he would have to quarantine in his room for 14 days, which was unthinkable for him. He could not have dealt with such imprisonment in an unknown place surrounded by strangers, and we crossed those homes which were rigidly enforcing the 14-day isolation off our list. How could we take this lovely but unwell and unhappy man to a place we couldn't see inside, and allow them to amplify his confusion and unhappiness by locking him up? You would not do that to an animal, let alone a much loved husband and father.

Eventually we found one home locally (out of about 15 we saw) who a) allowed us inside to see what it was like, and b) would not insist on the 14 days' purdah, so we arranged for him to be cared for there.

Nicci Gerrard describes what it was like for us when we took him there (theguardian.com/commentisfree/2021/may/02/why-did-the-government-take-so-long-to-back-down-on-this-care home-cruelty): 'One day in March, my friend, her sister and her mother drove her father to the home; when they arrived, he was bewildered and furious. His daughters had to stay outside. They watched as their mother hustled him indoors with his case and as the carers, who are kind people doing their hard, important job as well as they can, pushed him along. He was crying and shouting and they were helpless. His wife was allowed to unpack for him and then she, too, was obliged to leave and not return for several days. My friend cried for a week and she cries when she tells me her story; perhaps it is a story that will always make her cry. The suffering of people in care homes is also the guilt and grief of those who love them and are separated from them.'

Imagine if I had not been allowed in with him, but he had been wrenched away from me at the door, and if he was then locked up for two weeks. He would not have survived. Such patients are ILL, they have done nothing wrong and aren't going anywhere, whereas staff in the home come and go at will. The home were probably breaking the rules somehow, but they understood the profound cruelty involved in the 14-day quarantine requirement and we are grateful to them.

To people who have never been in this situation this might all sound uninteresting and unimportant, but for those of us trying to care for very ill and unhappy loved ones it is an abomination that this 14-day isolation policy was dreamt up in the first place and persists when people are visiting pubs and raves, singing at football matches and generally doing far more 'dangerous' things than my frail and lonely husband.

From Jane:

'Dad thought he'd done something wrong and was no longer loved!'

My father was diagnosed with Alzheimer's a few years ago, and in early March last year he and mum were muddling along quite well. He attended a day centre 3 days each week and this enabled mum to get a break from caring and get a few jobs done without dad shadowing her. The family also supported them with regular outings, sitting with dad if mum had, e.g. a doctor's appointment or errand, visits etc.

Then lockdown hit and dad wasn't able to go to his day centre, and lockdown rules massively reduced family visits. Dad thought he'd dome something wrong and was no longer loved! His condition deteriorated and in September he had a water infection and was hospitalised. He was isolated in a single room and initially no-one was allowed to visit. When mum eventually did visit, it was meal-time and dad's meal was a portion of rice – a food he would not usually eat. It transpired that he had been left with the menu-choice sheet but did not understand it. He may not have been able to read it as he has AMD [Age-related Macular Degeneration]. Clearly, the nursing staff had not considered his health other than the water infection, and failed to take into account his dementia and other issues.

After leaving hospital, his mental health had deteriorated considerably and this led to him being hospitalised again but this time under the Mental Health Act. He was in hospital from December to February and following his condition being stabilised, he was moved to a care home. Each move involved a period of isolation which was distressing both to him and mum (as well as the rest of the family!). Both in hospital and the care home, there were attempts to maintain contact using Facetime, but dad was unable to manage this himself and there were rarely staff available to support him. The 'contact' was therefore often distressing for all and not the helpful support that was portrayed in the media.

Under the latest restrictions we have been able to bring dad to my home to spend some time in the garden. There are occasional glimpses of dad's former self, but he has clearly suffered due to lockdown and successive periods in isolation. I think I can speak for the whole family in hoping that any future restrictions do not reduce family access to dad, as he so clearly benefits from contact, particularly seeing his great-grandson.

From a Daughter:

'And so another freedom - the ability to choose where mum lives, has been taken from us.'

Last summer we found a care home that was much more sympathetic and obliging with helping relatives keep contact with their families than the care home my mum is currently in. Mum had only been in her current home 5 months and, after trying hard to negotiate with her care home for better access to mum via window or garden visits, we decided to try and move her. It took a while to persuade social services to allow us to move her but unfortunately the care home we wanted to move her into couldn't accept her due to the 14 say isolation rule. Mum has Alzheimer's and would need one to one supervision during isolation and, understandably, they didn't have the staff to enable this.

Despite self funding and having financial power of attorney, we do not even have the ability to choose the care home mum is in, she is in effect trapped where she is and we are forced to follow the inflexible visiting arrangements of her current home. And so another freedom - the ability to choose where mum lives, has been taken from us unless the 14-day isolation rule for moving to a new home is removed.

Section 2

How the 14-day isolation rule damages people who need rehabilitation after a hospital stay

From Melanie (johnscampaign.org.uk/post/isolated):

'She had to isolate in a room she had never seen, in a place she didn't know, with people she had never seen before and no contact with us for 14 days.'

Our mum, Jean aged 91, was happily living an independent life in extra care housing with carers visiting daily. She was getting frail but her mental faculties were sharp. She went downhill during the past year with no visitors initially and then my brother fortnightly as her bubble. I saw her two or three times and noticed before Christmas that she was becoming increasingly confused.

Alan and Jean

A six week stay in hospital in February/March (where I was able to see her regularly and re-establish contact) resulted in a diagnosis of Lewy Body dementia and a recommendation that she entered a residential care home. She was taken in one afternoon with little notice - a phone call to my brother to say she was going. No choice, no visit, no say in the matter with the family. There was a Teams meeting where my brother was told what was happening. Then she just went.

My brother was allowed 45 minutes to get her into her room with very little in the way of possessions. Then he had to leave her. He cried all the way home. She had to isolate in a room she had never seen, in a place she didn't know, with people she had never seen before and no contact with us for 14 days. This is a person newly diagnosed with dementia. We went through hell trying to imagine how she felt. There have been a lot of tears.

This was in mid-March 2021 when the rest of the country was beginning to open up. My brother went to see her on day 8 because he thought this had been agreed. When he arrived he was told he should have made an appointment and was made to feel he was breaking the rules. He was told off when mum hugged him and given a strict half hour with no privacy. Mum's isolation continued for the full 14 days.

My brother was then told he could see her once a fortnight for 20/30 minutes. He has to make a 90 minute journey there and back. He was also told that he should try to settle her in while he was there. It takes mum a while to understand and settle to his visits and then she can't understand why he has to go so quickly.

When I became the second named visitor we were told to visit together once a fortnight or singly once a month. Needless to say we opted for the fortnightly visit but have since found out that, coming from separate households, we were not supposed to be doing this. Mum cried and hugged me when she saw me. This was not allowed. Her door had to stay open and we were interrupted three times by staff. We ended up with little quality time with mum.

Communication has been poor. I sent an email the day after her arrival, asking questions about laundry, possessions, meals etc. This was never answered. The 'Quality Care Manager' said it had gone to the umbrella company, she had never seen it. In the meantime we were in the dark about general day to day issues and have not received any information from the home. My brother has tried to book FaceTime calls but they never get back to him. Emails and phone calls are often met with no response. There are too many issues to list here and we have finally got a meeting arranged (after 7 weeks) which we hope won't encroach into our time with mum.

In the meantime, mum has lost even more weight, has become even more estranged from reality, has lost her feisty independence, has still not got her hair cut, we still don't know if she's had her second jab (they don't seem to know), is very tearful, has had nothing to do, is losing all ability to carry out things like turning on the TV or making a cup of tea because all this has been taken away. She has had to remove her jewellery, cannot have her nice glass vases, been told not to have too many clothes etc. etc. I feel she is becoming institutionalised. She has lost everything she holds most dear to her. This is not a life. Sometimes I wish she could die and be spared this. She didn't deserve it. The heartbreak for the family is just too upsetting.

Now, as mum's finances are being looked at, there is a chance she may need to move elsewhere. Will she have to go through all this again? What if she needs another hospital stay? Why is this being inflicted on her when it does such damage? Why are we prevented from supporting her and showing our love when she needs it most?

From Leighla:

'She was being offered a holding pen not rehabilitation; how could anyone blame her for declining.'

Leighla and her grandma

My grandma is 90. Until recently she has lived happily and independently at home.

Due to a fall, a difficult time in hospital and a rushed return home – she needed to go into a care home for emergency respite.

She is twice vaccinated, all residents of the care home are vaccinated. She did not enter until results of a lab test returned Covid negative – yet as per unreviewed guidelines she had to isolate alone in her room for 14 full days. There was no internet connection in her room to allow a video call. The window was too high for an outside window visit. Contact with staff was kept to the absolute minimum, showers were offered every 3 days and there were no activities apart from a TV and radio (which we provided).

When I saw her briefly on the day of her release (pre-arranged the week before) she was withdrawn and confused. I asked how her mobility was but she said she didn't know as she had barely been out of her chair. I had my two sons with me and only one could come in. I asked if my grandma could be wheeled to the front door to see her other great grandson in the flesh if he and my husband stood well back at the other end of the carpark. It was refused. After some persuasion it was agreed that she could see them from a distance but under no circumstances could the door be opened. My 3-year-old son was shouting across the car park and couldn't understand why she couldn't hear him. It was upsetting for everybody and we left in tears.

Less than 48 hours later an ambulance was called as she had signs of an infection in her legs. She was taken to hospital and treated. We were not allowed to visit during any stage of her hospitalisation including her 8 hour wait in A&E. We finally had a video call 1 week later only to realise she had no teeth in. She was extremely distressed – unable to eat and communicate properly. We were not notified there were any issues or asked to help find them. We spoke to the care home and dropped them off within 2 hours – we could have helped on day 1.

After she was deemed medically fit, the hospital could not secure the at home care package immediately and repeatedly asked my grandma to accept a transitional rehabilitation facility to clear the hospital bed. After clarification that this would again be straight into 14 days' isolation she repeatedly declined. She was being offered a holding pen not rehabilitation; how could anyone blame her for declining. As a direct result of the isolation policy, she was medically fit on a hospital bed for 6 days.

Eventually the care and at home nursing package was secured and my grandma returned home last week. She is extremely relieved and shaken by her experience. As I was leaving, she said 'I certainly won't make the mistake of going back there again'. It is so distressing that she deems it a better option to lie about her health than engage with services designed to help and protect her.

It seems unimaginable but true that this 28 day experience only scratches the surface of what people have been through over the last 14 months and are still facing today. We cannot turn a blind eye to the marginalisation and blanket removal of basic human rights for anyone in society, let alone the most vulnerable. The Government and Public Health bodies must act now.

From Rosemary
(johnscampaign.org.uk/post/death-in-isolation):

'The deterioration in her health was catastrophic. Deterioration for which a visiting GP could find absolutely no physical reason.'

An old friend (for whom I had POA and been the sole carer) was admitted to a care home for 2 weeks respite care - to give me a rest while a more appropriate package of support was obtained.

It was only after she had been admitted that I was informed that she would be placed in isolation for 2 weeks deprived of company and stimulation. Furthermore during that time she would not be allowed visitors. This in spite of the negative Covid swab that she had been required to provide to allow her transfer from the Royal Bournemouth Hospital.

Fit and well at 83

Yet an advertisement placed at the entrance to the care home since Christmas offers day care facilities. I am at a loss to know how this care home can reconcile their policy for day care clients with that for residents. [...]

At the time of my friend's admission she was still relatively fit and well in spite of being 83 years old. She was mobile (admittedly with the support of a rollator, used to going for a 40 minute walk with her dogs every day), alert, communicating, drinking and eating provided her special diet was provided. She was suffering from the early stages of an atypical Dementia but was enjoying life and when I agreed to her admission it was only because

I had been assured that she would be able to join in the activities and company of other residents of the care home.

18 days later she was dead.

The deterioration in her health was catastrophic. Deterioration for which a visiting GP could find absolutely no physical reason. The care home failed to alert me to the decline in her health and even then only voiced concern about her not eating and not having had her bowels open! But though I offered to bring in food that I knew she felt safe to eat the care home were not prepared to allow me a visit for a further 3 days. That visit was so disrupted and I was so worried by her appearance that I requested a further visit only to be told by the receptionist 'No, you've had your 30 minutes for this week.'

As it happened I had booked a visit at the time of her admission for 4 days later. In the meantime I tried to get her home but was prevented by the absence of a discharge package.

When I next was allowed to visit her (again through a plate glass window and using an intercom) she still had capacity to confirm she wanted to come home but it was also obvious that her health was failing so fast that there was no possibility of a recovery. So I requested a further visit only to again be told (by the Care Manager this time): 'No you've had your 30 minutes for this week.' That afternoon a visiting GP diagnosed that she was now in the 'final stages of terminal decline'. He could find no physical reason for this. I was informed that she would now require a palliative care package as a condition of being 'allowed' to return home to die. My friend had not lost mental capacity and I knew this was what she would have chosen. (It took me four days to make the necessary arrangements but they came three days too late.)

When I had heard what the doctor said, I again made a request for an urgent visit but it was met with the same response (from the care home manager): 'No you've had your 30 minutes for this week.' She would have liked spiritual comfort but this was not allowed. I asked to be contacted when death was imminent but needless to say this request was also refused - in spite of the regulations regarding 'end of life visits' that the Government had put in place in April 2020. She died alone and uncomforted.

Rosemary contrasted the treatment in the care home with the approach in hospital. There, her friend was required to isolate for 24 hours while the results of a swab were obtained. During that time, she was placed in a side ward, so was able to watch 'comings and goings', and have staff speak to her through the doorway as they passed by. Once the negative swab had been obtained, Rosemary was able to visit every day, so could monitor her condition. The hospital invited her to visit at a meal time and bring food appropriate for her special diet. Had she remained in hospital she would not have been refused end-of-life visits from her loved ones and would have been able to have a final communion.

Section 3

How people are damaged by repeated applications of the 14-day isolation rule

From Kimberley:

'The impact on my grandma's mental health and well-being cannot be underestimated.'

My 99-and-a-half-year-old grandma is currently in her 5th bout of 14-day quarantine. The reason for quarantine has mainly been returning from a stay in hospital. [...] What angers me the most is that people can return from abroad and only quarantine for 10 days. Why the disparity? My grandma has had both her Covid vaccinations and yet she is still faced with harsh restrictions. What was the point of the vaccinations, then, we have to ask ourselves?

The impact on my grandma's mental health and well-being cannot be underestimated. She is very weepy, her speech is very slurred due to few opportunities to speak to anyone, she said herself that this is not much of a life and she feels lonely. She cannot get a bath during this time, she cannot see the hairdresser during this time, nor can she interact with her peers in the dining room where she usually goes for her meals three times a day. She is simply left to sit in her chair for hours at a time, as she is reliant on carers to move her as she lost the use of her legs. [...]

I feel my grandmother is being kept alive with little regard for the actual quality of life. With only guidance in place, care homes do what they like; even though my grandma has a patio door, she is not even allowed to open it. Enough is enough. My grandma's life is almost over and it breaks my heart that she is spending her days like a prisoner.

From Hilary:

'She was recovering from a fractured pelvis so to leave her alone in a room was disgraceful and I'm sure not safe for her.'

My mum has had to isolate 3 times this last year after hospital admissions. Each time was for 14 days.

Mum has dementia, not only had she been in hospital without familiar faces then to be shut in her room for 14 days is nothing short of barbaric. She was also weak and disorientated from her hospital stay, how could this have been safe for her?

The first time this happened they moved mum to a room downstairs and the staff kept popping in to see her, the second time we paid an extra £1000 to have an agency carer to keep her company and to keep her safe for at least a few hours each day. The last time we were too scared to pay an agency worker that had potentially been in other care homes so the staff watched her the best they could. I offered to be tested and look after her but this was not allowed. She was recovering from a fractured pelvis so to leave her alone in a room was disgraceful and I'm sure not safe for her.

Mum didn't understand and she had been tested so I feel this shouldn't have happened at all. For us to go about our daily lives knowing mum was shut in her room broke my heart. I'm not sure I could do it and I haven't got dementia.

From Shirley:

'I never felt reassured in any way that the home were giving anyone isolating any further support to help them get through it.'

My dad has endured 4 x 14 days of isolation in his care home and has really struggled through every one of them. He has Alzheimer's and was confused enough in hospital, never mind the 14 days' isolation that followed every discharge.

My phone would literally ring off the hook as dad was lonely in his room and often forgetting and trying to leave his room, only to be told 'get back to your room', was a common occurrence. I never felt reassured in any way that the home were giving anyone isolating any further support to help them get through it. On one occasion I spoke to the care home manager and said my phone had been ringing nonstop on his first day of isolation, she replied: 'Well shall I take his phone off him?' I was horrified and said absolutely not! I asked, 'How are you going to help him get through isolation in his room knowing he struggles with it?' and her answer said it all: 'We are busy and have other residents to look after.' He got 2 jigsaws and someone went in once to play a game of dominoes with him.

I have to add that every hospital admission was as a result of issues with the care home staff. Getting Covid from 3 staff on October after it was well documented about infection control and 1 week after all residents were confined to their bedrooms after the outbreak. 3 further admissions after the staff refused to give him his inhaler even after I told them they were not giving him enough and had to ring his pharmacy GP and chest consultant they just didn't want to listen to me. So all these instances resulted in dad having a panic attack and chest pains then admission into hospital. So they caused every admission and practically no support in the 14 days of isolation that followed every time.

From Janice:

'He's still feeling low, having hallucinations, agitation, sadness, constant worry about family and feeling he's on his "last legs".'

My father Harry, aged 89, has been in the care home since middle of November. He is blind, has terminal cancer and has emphysema. On 3 occasions he has been admitted to hospital due to breathing difficulties where he was placed on oxygen and given antibiotics.

The night before the last admission, when he couldn't breathe properly, and where the nurse did not raise a concern, I spoke to the manager and questioned why dad couldn't be given the same treatment in the care home as I did not want him in isolation again, and requested she raise my concern with the doctor the next day. Her response was to talk about additional medication for his chest and said, 'sometimes oxygen causes more complications'. Really?

At midnight he was admitted to hospital and once more given oxygen and antibiotics. The doctor said the home should be treating him, not the NHS. Despite being back for a week there is still no oxygen in the home and no plan despite requesting a meeting with her to review. He is now in his third isolation period! The result on his return was him begging me not to remind the staff about it; when I told him he'd be in isolation his mood dropped. He's still feeling low, having hallucinations, agitation, sadness, constant worry about family and feeling he's on his 'last legs'.

I am today emailing the manager about putting a robust plan in place and asking for a test to be done so he can get his vitamin D from sunshine, not just a bottle. I believe he's now experiencing depression, which no doubt they'll want to medicate for!

From Elaine:

'Even prisoners are allowed 30 mins fresh air every day.'

I am contacting you as my father has just returned to his care home after a few days in hospital and is now required to isolate for 14 days. As an ECG I am allowed to visit him in his room which is something and I can try and keep his spirits up and encourage him not to give up!

However he is a very 'outdoors' person and he has been told he cannot leave his room to go outside in the gardens for some fresh air at all during this time. When I asked if he could sit outside with me when no-one else is about and away from the main area (the gardens are big!) I was told this was not possible as he has to go down a corridor to get outside. I feel that not getting any fresh air will effect his emotional well-being greatly - before he went into the home (18 months ago) he went for a walk every day of his life and spent most of his time outdoors. This last year has been extremely difficult for my father and just recently we have been allowed to take him round the local area for a walk which he has thoroughly enjoyed and my sister and I have noticed such a difference in his mental health and he is much more smiley. So it seems so cruel that he is once again being denied time outside, and worse out of his room. [...]

Another problem with the isolation is my father cannot understand why he has to stay in his room - on the TV and newspapers the rest of the world are now out and about socialising and going on holiday etc. and he is not even allowed to leave his room. He does not feel part of this world as it is so different from the one he is living in. [...]

My father is almost 93 and we just want to help him enjoy whatever time he has left. It seems so unfair and does not make sense that he has to have 14 days in isolation even when he has a negative test, is fully vaccinated and probably has antibodies as he had the virus earlier this year. If he had returned from a 'red country' he would only have to isolate for 10 days and the headlines in our local newspaper said there are no cases of Covid at the hospital. Even prisoners are allowed 30 minutes of fresh air every day.

From Sue:

'It literally broke my mum and broke my heart.'

It literally broke my mum and broke my heart. She was so affected by it that she hates being in her bedroom now even if I'm visiting her. She was beside herself yesterday trying to fight her way out of her bedroom. Its pretty much made her claustrophobic. I don't understand why it's 14 days. When she was taken from her mental health hospital it was 5 days' isolation after discharge and that was bad enough. Her care home made the sensible decision to 'release' her after 10 days as she was so depressed and upset. I'll never get over the trauma of looking at her through the window and not being able to do anything. It feels as though I've been through a trauma. It's affected her sleep as she hates the bedroom and as they've just reduced her 1-1 between 6am and 8am she's hurting herself trying to get out of bed when the rail is up.

From Laura:

'My mum called me relentlessly, sometimes in excess of fifty times a day, day and night, sobbing and begging me to go to her and let her out.'

My poor mum was forced to undergo 14 days' isolation upon admission to her nursing home last August. With dementia, it was pure torture. Mum was alone in a room she had never before set foot in, being cared for by a team of people she had never set eyes on wearing masks for a full fortnight. The WiFi connection in her room was unserviceable and the only means of contact was her mobile phone.

It tears me up to even recall those two weeks. My mum called me relentlessly, sometimes in excess of fifty times a day, day and night, sobbing and begging me to go to her and let her out. If she couldn't get hold of me, she'd leave phone messages (I had to stop torturing myself by listening to them), multiple times in succession and would then try my daughter or my brother, the next most commonly used numbers on her mobile. We all cried so many tears. I spent many, many hours on the phone every day talking to her and trying to calm and reassure her and trying my best to divert her attention from her plight.

My mum had always been an outdoors person, incredibly active and engaged, and being contained within her room and ensuite was hell on earth. I would try to distract her by recommending watching her television, but she was so confused she didn't even know how to turn it on. I would try to describe what a TV remote control looked like and talk her through step by step how to make it work so she could have a distraction, but more often than not to no avail. Her Alexa, which she had always had on at home playing music, wouldn't work without the WiFi connection, she couldn't sit still to read a magazine. I couldn't even visualise the layout of her room and describe where to find anything as I had never set foot inside the home, and still haven't to this day. The only escape was sleep, which was fitful and short-lived.

From Alison:

'It didn't cross our minds that she would have to suffer 14 days' isolation. If we had known this, we would have not agreed.'

My mother lost a filling so the home asked us to make a dental appointment. They did not mention the 14 days' isolation following the appointment. The dentist is a 2-minute walk/wheel from the home and is Covid secure. Because of this and mum's vaccine status it didn't cross our minds that she would have to suffer 14 days' isolation. If we had known this, we would have not agreed to the dental appointment. Mum was in no discomfort but she finds being by herself very hard.

It was therefore really distressing to find out only after the appointment about the isolation. Mum shouts and bangs when she is alone and gets very upset. She was very distressed by the isolation and didn't understand why she had to have all her meals in her room and couldn't go out. She became disruptive. In the end the home had to stop the isolation after 10 days (I think because of the disruption) after a negative test. The isolation made no sense to me as the home is 100% vaccinated (staff and residents) and staff are in and out of the home all the time. It feels cruel that people like my mum have to suffer it when they don't understand what is going on and feel punished when it happens to them.

From a Daughter:

'It's torture, it's inhuman and cruel and should not be happening in a civilised world.'

Mum is 66 has advanced Alzheimer's and has a DoLS [Deprivation of Liberty Safeguards] in place with no capacity. Over the last 14 months mum as had to isolate for 14 days due to Covid being in the care home and on another 3 occasions had to isolate herself due to showing symptoms and waiting for results. All these occasions were 5 days and all tests come back negative.

Mum's Alzheimer's makes her a pacer, she will walk the corridors for hours at a time, although during lockdown she has begun to slow down and has become a little unsteady on her feet and recently had a few falls. I believe this is due to a natural progression of her illness but also the amount of time she has been confined to her 4x4 room and the lack of stimulation and love and support from her family.

Mum is a loveable lady, she naturally smiles but she is very sensory, she loves touch and it's how she expresses her emotional needs and this has been taken away from her during isolation. Carers do not have the time to spend 1-1 with residents so they are spending most of their time in isolation alone, with no stimulation and 4 walls for company. My mum is 100% dependent on a carer; she cannot use a phone, she does not know how to turn on her TV or radio, and she has no concept of Skype.

Prisoners don't get treated like this so why elderly residents who cannot talk for themselves? It's torture, it's inhuman and cruel and should not be happening in a civilised world.

From Christine:

'She would stare blankly at the screen, was very monosyllabic and all she would say is "I'm a prisoner", "I have to stay in my room".'

I have had personal experience of how incredibly and irreparably damaging to residents' welfare this isolation policy is.

My own mum moved into a care home in Derbyshire in October 2019 and settled very happily. Her care has been exemplary and I have nothing but praise for how care staff have looked after mum during the pandemic. The care home has, however, followed Government guidance and isolated residents on several occasions. From October to November 2020 mum was isolated for 14 days on three separate occasions after members of staff tested positive.

I don't blame staff, particularly as last Autumn/Winter there were no vaccines. Mum has also been isolated after hospital admissions.

Mum was isolated in her bedroom, as were all residents. I call this 'solitary confinement', and, as you know, it is a punishment in prisons. Mum has dementia and is not able to read a book, complete a puzzle or follow a TV programme. All she could do was stare at the walls for 14 days. Staff do not have the time to spend engaging with residents in their rooms.

Mum needs the stimulation of activities that the home provides in the communal lounge and without this she sank into a deep depression.

She is still able to understand FaceTime so we were fortunately able to do this but, as you can imagine, sharing out iPads between all residents meant that these calls could not be frequent. When I did see mum on FaceTime the change in her demeanour, from when she wasn't in isolation, was devastating. She would stare blankly at the screen, was very monosyllabic and all she would say is 'I'm a prisoner', 'I have to stay in my room'. This was heart-breaking for me to hear, and it had a huge negative effect on my own personal mental health.

I simply cannot understand why residents are still being punished in this way. I personally feel that it is because of Government neglect to protect residents at the start of the pandemic with the result in huge numbers of deaths. This is currently in the news again, and I believe that when the handling of the pandemic is investigated, that this isolation of residents will also reflect very badly, quite rightly, on the Government. [...]

From Astrid:

'The only way I've been able to rationalise this situation is to compare it to a wartime footing where my loved one has been interned or captured by an enemy.'

Up until the pandemic began, typically I would take my mother home and care for her myself for a few days and nights, every six to ten weeks or so. This is what she had become used to along with our regular visits inside the care home.

I would track the separation's impact on my mum as follows: her basic confusion from March to June 2020, not understanding why she couldn't leave with me for a few days, this phase being followed by what to me appeared to be a depression from around June to October 2020, as she seemed to realise she wasn't going to be allowed to leave with me anymore. In October she contracted Covid and thankfully recovered, but from then on to Christmas the care home allowed NO CONTACT for families due to the outbreak. Our hopes rose in anticipation of a possible Christmas home visit, but were dashed again, and since then I feel she has become very withdrawn and distant, more often than not looking at the care worker rather than the phone screen if we are trying to have contact via telephones, very far from ideal for a person with dementia.

I fear she has lost all hope that she will ever be allowed to spend any meaningful time with me outside of the care home again. Occasionally she has managed to verbalise her discontent once saying 'this is not right' and on another occasion, 'Astrid, can you help me?'. I know it is difficult to really judge how a person suffering from dementia feels, but she is my mother and I can tell from her eyes if she is happy or sad, calm or anxious. I have begged the care home and social workers to let me take her home and care for her myself since the pandemic began, but her situation (she is on a DoLS) means I do not have the authority to do this.

In 15 months, I spent a TOTAL of 90 minutes with mum in person, this wearing full PPE. This situation has only eased in the last couple of weeks as the UK has opened up and the rest of its citizens enjoy myriad freedoms.

Last week under the latest guidance I was allowed to take mum to a restaurant with a terrasse. The weather was changeable and when there was a burst of torrential rain, I called the care home to ask if we could go indoors as the restaurant was spacious and social distancing rules seemed to be working successfully in my view, however, my request was declined. This is the typical response I have grown used to and although I appreciate the difficult position the care homes are in, their caution in this and, more particularly, the continued 14-day isolation rule, feels at best overzealous and at worst unnecessarily cruel. I have requested an Essential Care Giver status on numerous occasions and have had nothing but woolly responses.

The only way I've been able to rationalise this situation is to compare it to a wartime footing where my loved one has been interned or captured by an enemy (the UK Government) and jailed (care homes who are 'following orders') and I simply have no choice but to go along with the situation. The care homes will always choose the most stringent safety measures as along as the Government continues to cut them loose over indemnity.

All this being said, I am truly grateful to my mum's carers as I know she receives compassionate care, but the families of care home residents are beggars at the door and currently their loved ones are effectively prisoners.

Section 4

How the 14-day isolation rule discriminates against young people with disabilities, separates them from their families and damages them

From Karen:

'What she doesn't understand is why she is treated differently because she lives in a small care home.'

My sister is 48. She follows a football team, enjoys meals out, parties, theatre, holidays abroad, playing with the family dogs and has friends. Oh, and yes, she has a learning disability and is totally blind but that has never stopped her or us enjoying life. She understands we have all had to sacrifice a lot of the things we love and she is willing to do her bit. What she doesn't understand is why she is treated differently because she lives in a small care home.

She understands that vaccines give a high level of protection and that her friends, the people who support her and her family have all had two jabs. She doesn't understand why she is treated differently because she lives in a small care home.

She understands there are risks associated with mixing households, going on holiday and going to the pub. She understands she has a responsibility to others she lives with and comes into contact with. Much as she would love to, she is prepared to sacrifice some more to not to go the pub, or on holiday, or to a restaurant or to the theatre or to a football match. What she is not prepared to sacrifice is spending time in her family home with her parents or with my partner and I, as she has done every month for the past 30 years. She lives over 90 miles away from her family home due to lack of provision in her local area when she was 18 and looking to make her way in the world. She isolated after seeing our parents over Christmas. It was horrendous; having to ask to go to the toilet, eating meals on her own, denied fresh air, confined to one room. She understands and remembers. She is not prepared to do it again and neither are we. What she doesn't understand is why she is treated differently because she lives in a small care home.

When you read this, put yourself in her position. Think about this next time you are able to make a spontaneous decision to catch up with a friend for a drink. Spend an hour in one room and think about how that would feel after 14 days.

From William:

'The situation is affecting our mental health too with feelings of anxiety as to whether we will ever, in our remaining lifetime, enjoy family life with Emma again.'

My daughter is 38, has learning difficulties and is autistic with an associated severe communication disorder. She is cared for in a residential care home funded by social services and is subject of a DoLS certificate. Before the pandemic she would visit her family home monthly for a weekend and visit her older sister living 100 miles away twice per annum at Easter and Christmas.

We believe her mental health is suffering and this was forecast by her August 2019 DoLS. Quotes are:

'In the absence of any single fundamental facet of Emma's current care regime, she would be at extreme risk of rapid deterioration regarding her health and well-being' and 'any mood change must be monitored for and treated early and effectively to minimise the risk of an acute deterioration of her already impaired mental state'.

Earlier this year Emma was diagnosed with Covid-19 during a routine care home PCR test. As a result, although being asymptomatic, she was confined to her bedroom for 14 days. Her three co-residents also contracted Covid-19 about one week later but they exhibited classic symptoms and were in turn isolated in their individual bedrooms for 14 days. This meant that when my daughter, Emma, was released from isolation she was still isolated from her co-residents for a further week. The immediate consequence was that she refused to take part in the normal life of the care home without her friends e.g. she refused to have television on (a group activity) and sat around alone in the lounge and, although staff did their best for her, they were focussed on the three individuals isolating in their bedrooms.

Since then Emma and her friends have had both AstraZeneca vaccinations so they are well protected with antibodies both acquired by infection and introduced by vaccination. However, Emma's attitude to her family has become unpredictable particularly where it concerns mum and dad. [...]

On 5th April we made a garden visit to Emma. Her fellow resident had gone home for good reasons for the second time a couple of days beforehand. Emma was sullen, uncommunicative and would not give us her usual pretend hugs or blow a kiss. Not bright and cheerful and excited as she is normally.

On Wednesday, 14th April she suddenly broke off our weekly Skype call shouting and running away. Staff persuaded her to calm down and return to making the call.

More recently she has been physically sick twice coinciding with a parental visit. On the second occasion she refused to see us although we had arranged with her to take her out for a walk in a local park. She did finally agree to a garden visit but, although reasonably happy, she spent most of the hour on an exercise bicycle.

She has refused a home visit which we were willing to arrange because she understood the 14 days self isolation would apply. She became extremely distressed until we could reassure her via Skype that the choice was hers and she could stay in her care home until she decided to leave to come home.

It is clear that, as forecast, her mental health has been affected by a lockdown (which for her has lasted since March 2020) and fear of another 14 days of isolation if any rules are broken. Or she again contracts Covid-19 possibly from a care home staff member who does not suffer the same restrictions as Emma. She has become fearful and estranged from her family. [...]

I should add that my wife is 78 and I will soon be 80, suffering from an incurable kidney disease. We have both been vaccinated with the Pfizer vaccine and live in a small rural village. The situation is affecting our mental health too with feelings of anxiety as to whether we will ever, in our remaining lifetime, enjoy family life with Emma again.

From Sarah:

'There is no possible way he would stay in a room... the door would be broken down and this is not an exaggeration.'

Our son is severely autistic and lives in a care home in Essex. He lacks capacity and therefore is unable to comprehend what self isolation would mean. He would not understand why it was necessary to stay in his bedroom following an overnight visit to his family home.

To try to impose this upon him would cause a huge stress. He would become anxious and stressed which would inevitably lead to him self harming. There is no possible way he would stay in a room... the door would be broken down and this is not an exaggeration.

We fail to understand why, when he and we are double vaccinated and tested twice weekly, we are considered to be a huge risk. Especially when care home staff who are not all vaccinated are free to roam in and out of the care home and live normal lives once they are home.

From Ann:

'He lasted until day 11 and then he literally smashed up the house, hurting care staff too.'

Our son lives full-time at a specialist care home in Cheshire. He is 24 years old and suffers from a severe form of epilepsy called Dravet syndrome. He is profoundly learning disabled but cognitively aware and he is active, particularly outdoors. The last time he returned to the family home in Scotland for respite was on 16th October 2020. Ordinarily he would benefit from such respite 4-6 times per annum for two weeks each time. The October visit is the only time he has spent at home since lockdown began last March, his first Christmas and Easter away from mum and dad and his two brothers.

As you know, a 14-day isolation period is required on return to the care home. This is facilitated by a row of terraced properties with small gardens outside the care home campus. He lasted until day 11 and then he literally smashed up the house, hurting care staff too. He is 2:1 care by day. We insisted on 2:1 at night also whilst he was in isolation, which severely stretched the care home's resources, but with hindsight it was vital for his own sake and the sake of care staff.

He does not have the capacity to understand a 14-day isolation period. After 11 days he predictably expressed himself the only way he knows how: behaviours, which reflect his mental health. As a consequence we have been unable to have our son home for further respite. Instead we travel 4 1/2 hours to Cheshire fortnightly, there and back in the same day, and we spend 2 hours with him in a room with a partition screen. We consider this journey essential for his mental health.

None of this is acceptable but the isolation requirements are too cruel and too damaging. Unlike my mother who is 85 years old in a care home, our son is a young 24-year-old with high energy and a great joy for life that is being stifled by these restrictions. The long term consequence of being denied quality time at home with his family is yet to be determined.

From Morfydd:

'They cannot isolate in their bedrooms unless sedated and/or restrained; therefore, they have to be taken to separate isolation units.'

My own experience of this issue for young adults with learning disabilities is that they cannot isolate in their bedrooms unless sedated and/or restrained; therefore, they have to be taken to separate isolation units. This is a huge change of circumstances and routine for those who lack capacity to understand, and has resulted in much upset and very difficult behaviour, which can all too quickly become entrenched for that individual. It is important to remember that these individuals are not weak or frail but healthy young people with boundless energy, many of whom use physical movement and space as a means of regulating mood and maintaining wellbeing.

There are also the practical problems of availability and staffing of these isolation units so that even if one wishes to have a relative overnight then there is difficulty in returning that relative. In my own circumstances, I have had to be full time carer for weeks on end because a return cannot be accommodated. Over Christmas, when there was demand for these units, my own son remained in the family home for over six weeks; more recently, a similar problem resulted in a scheduled two weeks becoming five. This is completely exhausting for relatives, not to mention impractical in terms of trying to juggle other commitments; it is also not good for the individual, who has the problems of readjusting back into the care home environment after a lengthy time away. [...]

In fact, our son is far more exposed to Covid in the quarantine setting on his return with carers coming and going, not all of whom have been vaccinated.

From Helen:

'I have been intouch with Hayley's care home and they have said their hands are tied till the Government change their guidance.'

Our daughter Hayley is 29 and has always come home every other weekend for the last 10 years since residing in a care home, and comes away on holidays and longer stays at Christmas etc. Since the pandemic this has not happened, except for a 10 day stay at home in October 2020 and a week in September where a risk assessment was put in place by our daughter's care home. Myself, our daughter and my husband had PCR Covid tests done 2 days before we were due to pick her up for her home visit. On Hayley's return to the care home she had another PCR test done and if negative she could then join her peers, this wasn't nice for her but we could see why it had to be done. Why can't this be in place now as we have less cases of Covid than we did back in September and October 2020.

The 14-day isolation is not acceptable. It doesn't make any sense as carers can leave the care home, go to concerts, football matches, pubs, see their families who can do the same and see friends etc. who could potentially be a lot more at risk of bringing Covid into the care home than a loved one coming home for an overnight visit.

Time is precious and in a few years we will not be able to manage Hayley at home so we need to get the 14-day isolation abolished ASAP, if Hayley had to stay in her room for 14 days it would have a detrimental impact on her health and wellbeing she would withdraw and hit herself in the nose out of frustration as she loves the banter from the staff and the social aspect of being around people, doing crafts, planting, cooking all the usual activities she knew she would be missing out on if she were in isolation.

I have been in touch with Hayley's care home and they have said their hands are tied till the Government change their guidance.

Hayley's grandad passed away in January but we haven't told her because she needs to be at home with us so we can comfort and support her, we can't tell her in a visit and then just leave. Hayley has had her leg grazed on the cotsides of her bed and we think its because she's unsettled at times and wants to come home and sleep in her own bed.

Its Hayley's 30th birthday in July and we want her home to be able to celebrate this with her. All Hayley's Christmas presents are still on her bed at our home as she always comes home for 10 days over Christmas but this wasnt possible with Covid and we thought it wouldn't be that long after Christmas before we could have her home and celebrate Christmas later but this hasn't happened.

My husband was struggling with his mental health before Covid but now he's much worse, and all this is putting a strain on us all and there doesn't seem like there's any end in sight. This is not good for anyone not having the freedom to come home and visit your family.

From Jenny:

'[She] is very confused as to why she is different, she says, "Why different rules?"'

My daughter, aged 42, lives in a small care home with 3 of her friends. They all have a speech and language disorder, a couple of the girls have autism and they all have a learning disability. My daughter usually returns to the family home every 3 weeks or so and home for Christmas, Easter and holidays for a week or so. She has not been home now since March 2020. She relies on signing to communicate and needs signing alongside clear, precise speech to understand language and the situation.

She has had two sessions of 14 days in her room in isolation, which was incredibly hard for her. Firstly when a PCR test was lost and never had a result and secondly when she was diagnosed with Covid. This was spread to her via staff members, the only people she had seen! She is a very sociable young lady who loves being with her brothers and sisters.

She has become very anxious, feels she is in prison and scared of all the 'rules'. I have been allowed to visit outside now, but she is anxious the whole time. She desperately needs to be able to come home but I just cannot put her through another 14 days in her bedroom! Not even the house and garden like other people, but just a bedroom! It does feel like imprisonment.

When in her room, staff wear full PPE, so trying to hear and understand language behind a mask is bad enough, when she is isolated without her friends even worse. She is very aware that staff and others are allowed out to pubs, cafes and hairdressers without any 'punishment' and is very confused as to why she is different, she says, 'Why different rules?'

Very true. Why different rules for young ladies who happen to have a learning disability?

From Susan:

'Our daughter is at the level of a toddler.'

Our daughter is at the level of a toddler, and who would recommend a toddler, with a history of mental health problems, who struggles to understand what people are saying, who can't understand why she can't come home every three weeks, as she has done for the last 10 years, could only see their parents in PPE behind a Perspex screen and couldn't go to their parents' home and community unless they isolate for 14 days on their return?

I see that the Government changed the rules for people in care homes yesterday, so that they can go for trips outdoors, to day centres, educational settings and essential medical appointments. It is beyond my comprehension why theoretically young people with learning disabilities, autism or other neurological disorders can go to a further education college every day, where they would mix with hundreds of teenagers and young adults, who are unvaccinated, may not be socially distancing and going to pubs, restaurants, people's houses, etc. every week, but they cannot go indoors in their parents' home, when their parents are likely to be fully vaccinated - unless they self isolate for 14 days, on their return to the care home?

From Jaishree:

'The initial fortitude Riya seemed to show is now dissipating away and the care home staff are reporting lots of behavioural issues such as bed-wetting, repeatedly banging the door to her room, screaming at the staff.'

My only child, Riya, is 38 and has severe learning disabilities with particular problems in expressive language. This means, essentially, that she has the mental age of a 2-year-old or less and has not been able to understand at all this ghastly pandemic and lockdown.

Riya moved into her care home twenty years ago - a cheery, well-run place - and, though she knows it is her primary home, she has always thrived on home visits to us every other weekend. She also adores long holidays to India where we go once a year to spend time with her two elderly grannies as we have no family in the UK.

Of course, lockdown changed everything in March last year and we all took in our stride the dramatic developments, including (rather amazingly) Riya. She has no understanding of why things changed but something about being in the same boat as everyone else must have led to her accepting the many months that passed without seeing us or coming to our house. Through Christmas and Diwali and birthdays, we managed with video calls and had a joyous fortnight with her at home when things opened up briefly in the summer. Then came the second and third lockdowns and, when visiting was finally allowed this year, Riya's care worker persuaded me to make a tentative attempt in the hope that it would reassure her to see me in the flesh.

I was quite willing to be given the Government's much-touted lateral flow test and await the results sitting in a cold & rainy garden (another visit was on-going in the tiny visitors' pod), if it was going to offer Riya any comfort at all. However, given the formal setting, the compulsory PPE, our inability to hug or even touch each other, the constant presence of a care worker and a timer counting down our half-hour together, it was a joyless affair. Worst of all was the mask that Riya had to wear which robbed me of all the facial cues I am usually reliant on to understand how Riya is feeling. Watching her eyes dart around seemed to indicate utter confusion and I have no idea if she was even happy to see the box of Kristy Kreme doughnuts I had taken along for her house.

I got the impression Riya was completely bewildered when our time was up and I stood up and walked away without her. On the train back, I tried to console myself by imagining and hoping she would have been distracted away from thoughts about me while handing out doughnuts to her friends but this was probably a vain hope. I feel sure she would have a much stronger reaction were I to try visiting again, by which time she would probably have worked out that it was only going to be for a short while. I certainly don't think I could bear it if she started to scream or sob when I left and so visiting her care home isn't something I'm likely to be trying again. It may also have inadvertently set off a regretful chain of events, although I could not be entirely sure of this.

Very worryingly, the initial fortitude Riya seemed to show is now dissipating away and the care home staff are reporting lots of behavioural issues such as bed-wetting, repeatedly banging the door to her room, screaming at the staff and throwing things around. She desperately needs to return to the familiarity of home visits as the care managers agree with us that our visiting the home would only make her feel worse.

It is this that the Government fails to understand as they seem to think it acceptable to lump all care home residents into a group that thinks and behaves as one. While going in to hold the hand of a dying relative may bring immense comfort to some, it can have the most damaging effect on one with Riya's needs. Increasing the numbers of visitors from two to five is just as meaningless for people in our situation.

It's equally mystifying that ministers seem willing to ignore the risks caused by care staff returning to their homes every day while focussing so fiercely on the risks that may be caused by residents going home to spend valuable time with their families. Expecting that someone with Riya's limited faculties would be able to self-isolate for 14 days on returning to her care home is laughable. For one, she needs physical help with practically everything. Besides, she would simply break the door down if anyone attempted to lock her in!

Also, what logic are the Government bringing to allowing young, unvaccinated people the freedom to hug and socialise and spend overnighters in each other's houses while continuing to keep our children locked up? Riya and all her fellow residents have received both vaccinations, as have we as my husband and I are in our 60s. Whatever happened to our 'Right to Family Life', supposedly enshrined in the Human Rights Act?

Section 5

How the 14-day isolation rule disrupts family lives as they have to choose between not seeing their children or subjecting them to the 'torture' of isolation they can neither understand nor endure

From Jill (johnscampaign.org.uk/post/we-decided-we-had-to-get-her-home-as-soon-as-possible):

'Even prisoners aren't subjected to such isolation and in fact, I read an article recently where in America, solitary confinement for longer than 14 days is now classed as torture!'

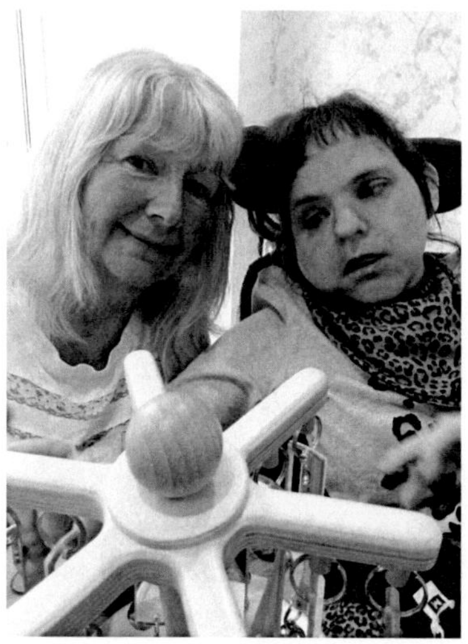

Jill and Amy

My 36-year-old disabled daughter, Amy, lives in a care setting. In normal times she comes home every weekend Saturday to Monday, but of course this has not been possible since last year. We had her home for 2 weeks in September when all she needed before returning was a negative PCR test which we organised. In early November she was home again for one week and the same applied. The only requirement was a negative PCR test. No problem.

At Christmas we were planning her return home when, at the last minute, the care home said that the rules had changed and that she would now need to quarantine in her room for 14/15 days on return. We made the difficult decision not to have her home, partly because the first round of vaccinations were due at the home early January and we didn't want her to miss it, but mainly because of the effect isolation would have on our sociable daughter. Her care home room is tiny with just about enough room to wheel her chair around the bed, the TV she has is high up on the wall (Amy is severely visually impaired) and doesn't even work and the only entertainment and stimulation she would have would be the iPad which we had bought her.

When we were allowed the single person visits I was the chosen one (which broke her dad's heart) and I found these visits, which were in her bedroom, deeply upsetting. She became upset when I left her and I cried all the way home. We decided we had to get her home as soon as possible. The care home staff were very helpful as they too agreed that Amy needed to be home and, after a best interest assessment, a mental capacity assessment, a consultation with PHE and Amy's social worker, and after us agreeing to their risk assessment we finally got her home, supposedly for two weeks.

Unknown to them we had NO intentions of taking her back until this cruel, inhumane, unnecessary lengthy quarantine changed.

We have now had her home for four weeks and nothing has changed. My husband and I are both in our sixties, we have put our lives on hold; we are physically tired (Amy is doubly incontinent and needs lifting for every change) and sleep deprived but we are determined to see this through. Even prisoners aren't subjected to such isolation and in fact, I read an article recently where in America, solitary confinement for longer than 14 days is now classed as torture!

The care home manager is very sympathetic but all she says is that they are following PHE guidelines and that they must protect the four other residents in Amy's bungalow.

Just for the record, my husband and I are both retired, nobody else lives with us, we have both had both vaccinations (as has Amy), we're both doing LFD [Lateral Flow Device] tests twice weekly, we take Amy for rides on her own personal transport and have picnics in her bus, we only walk outside where it is very quiet, we haven't been in or near a shop, pub, cafe, we've had no visitors to the house and haven't been near or inside anyone else's house. What more do they want?

I'm sure those four other residents are much more at risk from the staff, many of whom have young families at school and husbands going out to work and granny and grandad helping with childcare. We haven't seen our other daughter or our young grandsons since we brought Amy home. Why should we have to choose between our children? I don't think anyone else has to now.

Amy seems happy at home but I worry about how she will be when she does go back. She must be missing her friends and maybe getting a bit fed up of just the two of us! What's best for her, and us, is a mixture of the two settings, as we had before, but the 'powers that be' seem to have forgotten all about the needs of these human beings. We thought Amy was settled for the future when we found this care setting only 3 short years ago and, although nobody could have predicted this awful pandemic, we and the 'powers that be' DO have the power to choose how we react to it.

From Madeleine:

'She agreed she would do the isolation again but she keeps changing her mind.'

My 46-year-old daughter lives in a residential home with seven other similar adults. They were in lockdown since beginning of March 2020. Catherine had periods of extreme anxiety, crying etc. because she couldn't get home. I brought her home last August for two months but she knew she would have to do two weeks isolation. It was hard but she did it.

Then in January all the residents and most of the staff got Covid due to a staff member being exposed to it. Again they all had to be isolated in their rooms, so hard. Catherine can use her mobile phone so that was a godsend.

So we got to Easter, Catherine not having been home for 5months. She was getting terribly upset. None of them had even been out except in the garden. I decided to bring her home and she agreed she would do the isolation again but she keeps changing her mind. It's daunting for anyone but her comprehension is limited so this is all frightening. She misses her friends and her life of going to day centres, discos, outings etc. If only the Government would stop treating all care homes the same.

From Freda:

'She has been home since April this year and couldn't possibly cope with another 14 days of isolation and so will not go back until this draconian rule is removed.'

Our daughter Emma stays at the same home as Catherine. Emma has experienced isolation when a member of staff brought the disease into the home. She found isolation extremely difficult and was phoning us at nearly every hour of the day. It had a serious effect on her mental health.

She has physical problems as well. So she went all the 14 days without a shower as staff could not help her when she had Covid.

She has been home since April this year and couldn't possibly cope with another 14 days of isolation and so will not go back until this draconian rule is removed. Everyone in the home is fully vaccinated, we have been ultracautious whilst she has been at home, we are fully vaccinated so why can't some combination of testing and minimum isolation be used? The poor way that Covid was handled last year in care homes would seem to have made them adopt the approach that if we don't take any risk at all then we won't be caught out again. Meanwhile their staff go here, there and everywhere as they like and just rely on tests to keep the disease out. It doesn't make sense.

From Niall:

'We do not know what the future holds for him or us, but we knew that he would no longer be able to cope with the restrictions in place.'

We collected our son from his care home on Friday, after he finally decided he no longer wanted to live there. We do not know what the future holds for him or us, but we knew that he would no longer be able to cope with the restrictions in place.

For much of lockdown he was at home with us, but returned on April 12th to, of course, 14 days of complete isolation in his room. Since then he has been out twice with a member of staff to an open space. On both times he has been required to change clothes completely on return to the care home. He has been refused permission to sit outside at a pavement café this week to have a drink, as one example of how things have not changed since the general easing of lockdown on 17th May.

Although we have been making a permitted one hour visit per week, we did not fully realise the extent of the impact on his life until we collected him on Friday. It was sad to see a man normally so sociable and ready to go out so amazed at seeing people going around their normal lives in the community, albeit taking precautions. Friday was spent punctuated with regular questions such as 'Will we be allowed to do this/that?' We repeated the message that he was now free to make his own decisions and did not have to refer to a higher authority before doing things. This is from someone who is recognised as having full mental capacity and is indeed a university graduate.

From Eve:

'We would rather our own health suffer than see him tortured again.'

In February of this year my son Jon (41) started to display symptoms of Covid infection and was immediately confined to his room in his residential care home, Whitehatch in Horley, Surrey, run by 'Acheive Together' It took 3 days for the test results to come back negative.

I telephone Jon every day and I could tell from the start he was not happy. He was quiet and sullen, most unlike the witty chatterbox he is. I took to daily Skype calls which were monitored by a member of staff in his room. Seeing him this way brought tears which I could not hide from him, even as hard as I tried, this obviously affected him as he would also start to cry.

We learned that when left alone he would try to escape from his room and had to be physically restrained on a number of occasions. Other residents would knock on his door asking him to come out (they could not understand either). Jon is very fortunate in that he has a fully glazed door into the garden however seeing people outside was akin to being taunted.

A normally very laid back individual, Jon resorted to lashing out when the frustration overcame him. The torture was threefold, him enduring something he could not comprehend, a mother having to watch his deterioration and a father who had to handle my anger and frustration as well as his own. We have been married almost 50 years, have grown strong together and will no doubt shake off the name calling and unpleasantness.

Following enforcement of the 14-day rule that seemed to surface in April, we have removed him from the care home until such time as this inhumane requirement is lifted. We are both approaching 70 and the physical side of looking after a grown man is beginning to tell but we would rather our own health suffer than see him tortured again.

Section 6

The lengths people have to go to to avoid 14-day isolation rule

From Fiona:

'We are trapped in this cycle of nonsensical, draconian and inhumane "guidance".'

So, here's a slightly different take on how the current guidance not allowing an overnight family stay was in reality on the weekend of 21st/22nd May:

Ann, aged 58, is severely disabled due to Athetoid Cerebral Palsy and is wheelchair dependent, unable to speak, relies on an eye gaze communication device and requires full assistance with all aspects of her personal care. Ann usually visits her sister and partner's home every third weekend and stays Fridays to Sundays. During these visits, as well as seeing her other sister, nieces, nephews and friends, Ann routinely has a home visit from a neurophysiotherapist and attends a local hydrotherapy pool for a 2:1 hydro session, as well as going out for coffee and copious amounts of clothes and shoes shopping! The loss of these weekends 'home' has had such a detrimental impact on Ann as well as her sister who looks forward to their quality time together and giving Ann a change of scene and a sense of family/social life beyond her residential setting that makes her life worth living. [...]

When the Government changed its guidance from 17th May 'allowing' residents of care homes to go off-site in very controlled and restricted circumstances, Ann was 'allowed' to go out for the day with her sister and so, on Friday 21st May, Ann's sister arrived at the care home, took an LFT test, Ann also took an LFT test, they then went home for a few hours, sat in the garden with Ann only legally allowed to go in for attending to her continence needs. Before returning to the care home, both Ann and her sister were required to do another LFT test and report the outcome and could then go back. On Saturday 22nd May, Ann and her sister followed the same routine, taking their LFT test total to 4 each in 30hours... Please can anyone tell us how Ann being 'allowed' to stay overnight on the Friday would have actually increased the risks?

The main risk from those two crazy days was that Anns' sister would die from exhaustion of doing 4 return trips to her sister's care home, a total of 8 hours driving over those two days in addition to providing extensive care both physically and emotionally.

It cannot be right that 4 LFT tests are required in such a short period. Care homes appear to be in chaos as they struggle to follow Government guidance to the letter.

So, next weekend we face doing the same crazy process all over again. Even if the care home said OK, let Ann stay overnight, she could not mentally cope with the 14-day isolation and so we are trapped in this cycle of nonsensical, draconian and inhumane 'guidance' which feels to have become firmly embedded in our society as 'law'. It has to stop.

Section 7

How a few people have defied the 14-day isolation rule

From Amanda:

'It has driven her literally mad. She repeats the same phrases over and over again: "I've got nobody" "Nobody comes" "Where are the people?" "There's nothing. Absolutely nothing".'

My mother is bed-bound, has advanced Alzheimer's and is classed as EoL [End of Life]. She has been effectively isolated in her room for 1.5 years and the impact on her has been absolutely devastating. This was hugely exacerbated by visiting restrictions.

Up until March 2020, she had regular and prolonged visits from family but during the pandemic it was just 1 hour per week, and for almost two months (not consecutive), she had no visits as the home had outbreaks. Her cognitive decline has been significant even considering her existing condition. It has driven her literally mad. She repeats the same phrases over and over again: 'I've got nobody' 'Nobody comes' 'Where are the people?' 'There's nothing. Absolutely nothing'.

I have been fighting to take her out of the home and look after her myself since returning from my home in Italy in March 2020 to look after her but have suffered obstacle after obstacle, despite having LPA [Lasting Power of Attorney] for Health and Welfare. Until early April, I was travelling 7 hours round trip to see her every week for just one hour. After some battle, I was granted ECG status and visits and duration increased. What I witnessed during those visits at the home was beyond shocking and, due to the urgency of getting her out of there, I fought for her to be moved into nursing care closer to me. [...]

I called seven dementia nursing homes within a 50-mile radius, six of which said my mother would need to be strictly isolated for 14 days with no family visits. Each of the six told me that after the 14 days, their visiting policy would be 30 mins max per week even for EoL - unless within last days of life. None of the six had even heard of essential care giver status.

Fortunately one of the homes had a completely different approach. My mother is now in day 10 of isolation from other residents but has been supported throughout the transition to the new home by myself. The manager has been both compassionate and practical and allowed me unlimited access.

Initially, my mother refused all drink and food from staff, as I feared would be the case. However, with unlimited access, I have been able to assist with meals and medication and helped to ensure that my mum remains well-hydrated throughout the day.

Gradually, my mother is settling in and beginning to accept assistance from staff. Most importantly, she has received the one-to-one emotional support, care, and stimulus she needed from her family. The transition has been very disorienting and frightening for her but, had she had to isolate from family for 14 days, she would have felt completely abandoned, refused sustenance and died within days. Of that I am sure.

From Julie:

'When the manager of the new home told me my mother would have to isolate for 14 days I said in that case she wasn't moving there.'

In February this year my mother had to move to a different care home when she requested financial support from the local authority. Her social worker had assessed her as requiring one person with her at all times when mobilising. She also identified that my mother's condition meant she could not remember how to use an emergency call button.

When the manager of the new home told me my mother would have to isolate for 14 days I said in that case she wasn't moving there. The manager was rather taken aback but did accept that my mother would be at high risk of falls if left alone as she would not remember not to walk and would be unable to call for help, so would almost certainly try to walk unaided if she required the toilet.

The home she was moving from was completely Covid free so it was agreed that my mother would undergo a PCR test before the move and a lateral flow test on the day of the move. She was then allowed to mix with other residents from day one.

Not all but surely many of our loved ones are equally unsafe if made to isolate. Homes should be made to explain how they are going to mitigate against risks identified. I know this is not the sort of example you are seeking but it might help someone to challenge an isolation order.

Having said all that I think it is criminal to make any resident isolate.

From Linda:

'She has been isolated for a total of 65 days in 15 months.'

My mum was used to going out of the care home at least 3 times a week and seeing her children, grandchildren and great-grandchildren before lockdown. She is mentally alert.

From March till Christmas the only time she left her care home was to go to hospital for 2 days and then for a check up. Visits varied from visiting her on a decking, shouting through a double glazed door, window visits, to no visiting at all, then 1/2 hr visits in designated room with full PPE. As mum is very deaf all these were horrendous.

Mum said it was worse than being a prisoner... prisoners got visitors and had access to fresh air! During this time the home had 3 positive tests resulting in 3 lots of 14 days' isolation, where mum had no exercise, no fresh air, no company, no stimulation. Prisons are told no more than 72 hours isolation.

At Christmas mum was desperate to GO OUTSIDE and see grandchildren and great grandchildren. As mum was of sound mind I argued to bring her home, because of further lock down, she was only allowed a day at home. The price she paid was a further 10 days in isolation. In March she was 100 years old. Again I argued bring her home so we could celebrate this special birthday! She came home for 6 days. On return she had to isolate a further 14 days. [...]

She has been isolated for a total of 65 days in 15 months. During this last period she became very depressed, ringing us on her iPad crying, refusing to talk because she said she had nothing to talk about, and wishing she could have fresh air and feel the sun on her face and saying this was no life! In desperation I brought her out of the care home for her and my sanity. I have no downstairs bathroom or bedroom. But we coped! Mum's mobility had seriously declined. She had only been walking from the bed to the bathroom.

Eventually I found a lovely care home that did a test at my house, allowed her to look round before going in, no isolation!! Visits in and out. She is settling well. Mum lived through the Second World War. She wonders how future historians will judge this period.

"I worry, sometimes, that care homes have taken things too far"

Listening, Learning and Making a Change

'What am I being punished for?' Helen's 98-year-old mother asks her. Because everyone knows that being sent to your room and confined there without company, exercise, occupation or love is a punishment, and if it's continued for 14 days, you must have done something very bad indeed. The answer is obvious: Helen's mother is being punished for being old and likely to die. I have rarely seen anything so fatuous on TV as the Government adviser at his lectern, gesturing at a slide that said 90-year-olds were at greater risk from death than any other population group.

An acute respiratory illness is more likely to be a problem for people whose lungs are weak. So here's another good idea – deprive them of sunshine and fresh air in the name of safety. It is hard to forgive the guidance writers of 2020 who promised that guidance on visits out would be published 'shortly', failed to act on this, then copy-pasted the identical sentence into the next two iterations in September and October, by which time summer was gone.

Occasionally commentators, sensitised to the reality of discrimination against older people living in care homes, have said 'If those care homes were full of children, there'd be a public outcry'. But there *are* homes full of children: their bodies may be 20, 30, 40 years old but some of them have the understanding of toddlers. I am fed up with the word 'heartbreaking'; it is excruciating for parents (like Tony and Debby on the Crowd Justice video crowdjustice.com/case/care homes) to hear their adult child promising to be good, begging to be 'allowed' home. Many such parents can't visit because of the acute distress their children feel on realising they are not going for their weekends home. Joan's son Robert is 43 and has reverted to the crawling stage. He cannot verbalise his distress so he bites his arm until it is red and sore. Robert needs dental treatment at the moment but this would involve a hospital admission and 14 days' isolation. The guidance calls this 'self-isolation'. For Robert, it means being strapped in his chair with a chest restraint, lap restraint and his legs secured. For 14 days.

Are the Government advisers who write this guidance callous, wicked or simply ignorant? Dr Eamonn O'Moore, the person being introduced by the Care Minister to the Joint Committee on Human Rights as responsible for care home visiting out guidance, is also responsible for prisons. What does he know of the distress being expressed by Jaishree's daughter Riya through bed-wetting, door-banging, screaming and throwing things? Yesterday I asked Robert's mother Joan what she would like to tell the Care Minister. 'I'd like to tell her how frightening this is. One false move by us – letting him inside other than to change his nappy, for instance; one unavoidable hospital admission and he will suffer, strapped down in isolation for 14 days.'

There is no representation on the Government committees for people who live in care homes or their families. When the Government says it has engaged with 'stakeholders' to develop its guidance, this does not include the people who live in care homes or those who love them. And the people who pay the most for what they increasingly describe as their 'incarceration' have the smallest voice as they can be evicted without redress.

After fruitless attempts last year to enable family voices to be heard and, especially, the needs of people living with dementia to be understood we began to communicate with the Government through lawyers. John's Campaign is not a charity and does not have money so this would not have been possible without the generosity of people who contributed to our first Crowd Justice site (crowdjustice.com/case/government-guidance-has-failed-care homes). Now we have a second site supporting legal action to enable people to leave their 'homes', without being punished for it. The Government lawyers assure our lawyers that what is happening is not false imprisonment, as adults with mental capacity are always free to leave – they just can't come back unless they are prepared to quarantine for 14 days. One dignified centenarian with the ingrained stoicism of the WW2 generation wept as she told her son she had begun to feel 'like a leper'.

The Government lawyers give our lawyers a list of the people they say helped draw up this guidance. We are surprised at some of the names. Kate Lee, CEO of the Alzheimer's Society, takes to Twitter: 'Just to be clear @alzheimerssoc doesn't support this. The self isolation period is pointless, cruel and has no evidence behind it. We have been joining everyone else who is calling for it to be totally removed and will continue to do so.' Other friends from #OneDementiaVoice agree. Ruth Eley writes 'At TIDE – Together in Dementia Everyday – we have heard many stories from our carer members of the cruelty of the enforced isolation of those they care about and desperately want to continue to visit and support. [...] They could be those extra pairs of hands, alongside the hard-pressed paid care staff, able to provide the individual care for residents that is so essential for quality of life and personal well-being.' She's right; Elaine's testimony shows that using the Essential Care-Giver scheme can mitigate harm. But this scheme is not yet mandated: so only the good care homes use it – and the harm of 14 days enforced isolation for people whose only crime is that they have moved into a care home, moved out of hospital or have visited inside their family home – should not exist.

Ashley Bayston, Founder and Chair of the Lewy Body Society and human rights lawyer, writes: 'The moral strength of a society can only be measured by how it treats its most vulnerable members. The Lewy Body Society stands strongly with John's Campaign about the inhumanity of the 14-day isolation rule.' Jenny's daughter asks her mother: 'Why different rules?' The answer is because you live in a care home, because you're disabled. In equality-speak everyone who lives in a care home, whether old or young, with or without mental 'capacity' has at least one 'protected characteristic' under the Equality Act. This should not mean that it's okay to shut them in their rooms for 14 days, to 'protect' them. There's an odd shift of language happening here. Surely people who are disabled, ill, frail should be treated better not worse? At the very least, 'reasonable adjustments' should be made so they can enjoy the same opportunities as the rest of society. The danger of lumping unique people together as 'the vulnerable' is that they can too easily be seen as lesser.

In the worst places (see Rosemary's testimony) this comes close to abuse and in others (see Astrid's) adherence to the Government guidance allows the petty 'jobsworth' unkindnesses that have been such a shameful feature of care home life. Why did Astrid feel she had to ring and ask 'permission' to take her octogenarian mother in to shelter from the rain? Because she was afraid that if she were discovered, she would lose her visitor access and her mother would be put into 14-day solitary confinement. And why did the care home refuse?

We know from our friends on the John's Campaign care home steering group how hard their job has been – and, too often, how much harder the Government guidance has made it. Government may say it's only guidance, not law. Raina Summerson, CEO of Agincare, speaks for many when she explains the pressure from local authorities, CQC, insurers to follow the Government guidance to the letter (youtu.be/jLzIYLtSF3s). One manager, combing the regulations to write a risk assessment that would allow one of her residents to walk to his bank to sign forms, said she sometimes feels she is party to a 'war crime'. You may not like words such as 'cruelty', 'imprisonment', 'discrimination' and 'enemy'; you may dislike the cartoons that we have used. Please contrast these with the loving 'normal' people in the photos and ask what has gone wrong if these people are using such words. Rachel Johnson, listening to Jean's experience in conversation on LBC, reacted spontaneously; 'You know when the Covid enquiry is going to start in the spring, they could judge that this actually amounts to torture.' (soundcloud.com/johns-campaign/14-days-isolation-why)

Adam Purnell, Care Quality Lead for Kepplegate Care Home writes: 'Reading this booklet sobers you to the true extent of the cruel approach to 'protecting' our most vulnerable living in care during the pandemic [...] There was a better way to manage this crisis and for months I had attempted to share my approach with those in possession of the power and authority to bring around change.' Adam's approach involves constant, mutually respectful discussion between residents, relatives and staff, confronting the problems together. He has enabled regular indoor visiting since last June and kept out Covid.

Listening could still make a difference. This week the British Geriatric Society listened to some of these personal accounts of harm done by the 14-day isolation rule, recognised the Human Rights concerns, looked at national data and, on 3rd June, put out a statement amending their earlier advice (bgs.org.uk/policy-and-media/bgs-supports-change-to-14-day-isolation-policy-for-care home-residents): 'Whilst recognising the ongoing need to protect care home residents from Covid, the BGS calls on national public health bodies to review, and remove at the earliest possible opportunity, restrictions on the movements of residents, including the requirement at the point of admission that they isolate for 14 days.'

The Government could answer that call now, today, if they had the humility and humanity to listen to the people in this book. Meanwhile I suppose we have to wait for the Judges to decide. Please don't forget our CrowdJustice page (crowdjustice.com/case/care homes).

Julia Jones, Author of *Beloved Old Age and What to Do About It* and Co-founder of John's Campaign

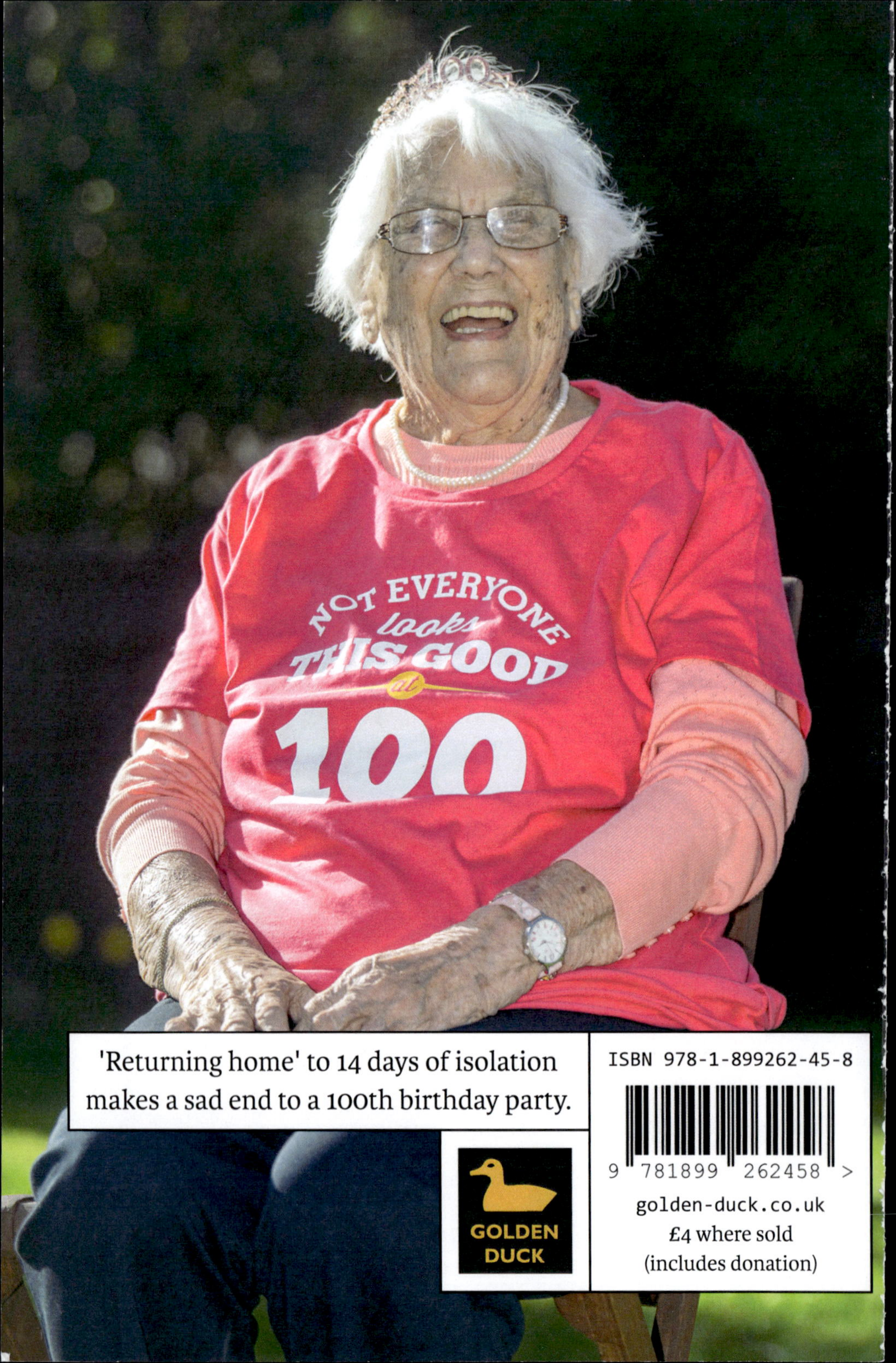

'Returning home' to 14 days of isolation makes a sad end to a 100th birthday party.

ISBN 978-1-899262-45-8

golden-duck.co.uk
£4 where sold
(includes donation)